Accessing the Akashic Records

A Practical Guide to Healing, Clarity, and Empowerment

Dr. La Toya Davis

CHI Publishing
Tallahassee, Florida

ISBN: 978-1-959406-14-3 (Paperback)

Book edited by:
Darlene Adams of 5th Dimension Agency
Heather Asiyanbi of Pens & Proof Publishing

CHI Publishing PO Box 7518
Tallahassee, FL 32314

www.thechipublishing.com

For information on special purchases, bulk orders or product support visit thechipublishing.com.

Dedication

There is nothing greater than being able to show up exactly as you are. I have had the privilege of a lifetime of people who have loved me as I was. That love gave me the freedom to investigate where I was not actually showing up as my most full and authentic self. That investigation is what hooked me to the Akashic Records, and for that, I am forever grateful.

For holding space and allowing me to take up space:

My mom, Andrea Mickens Davis.

My dad, Retired Lieutenant Colonel Walter Davis.

My best friend, Latora Francis.

My best friend, Walter Jones.

My babies, Ayah and Azariah Davis-Craig.

For praying for me and wrapping me in the highest energetic vibration:

My godmother, Yayi Nancy Samuels.

My godfather, Tata Kwame Azalius Ross.

For trusting me to do this work:

ArchAngel Metatron, the Masters, Teachers, and Loved Ones of the Akashic Records

Egbe Aiye, Egbe Orun

To all my previous clients:

Thank you for continuing to ask for more and push me past my comfort zone.

Contents

Transmuting Energy for Transformation: Clearing and Resetting in the Akashic Records

Weaving the Threads of Wisdom: Integrating the Akashic Records into Your Spiritual Journey

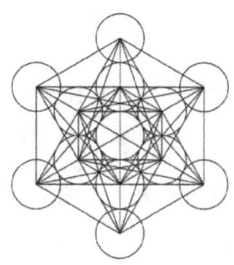

Introduction

"My soul is always pushing me to the highest and greatest version of myself. My job is to quiet the ego and follow the urgings. The Akashic Records help me do that." - Dr. La Toya Davis

I want to share a story with you. One day in 2019, while exploring my Akashic Records, I felt a strong nudge to grab a pen and paper. Now, I've got to be honest, despite being a coach and teacher who champions the benefits of journaling, I rarely brought pen and paper into my own meditations. But, as always, I trusted my intuition and followed the urging of my spirit.

On this particular day, like many before, I simply opened my Records and asked, "What information is there for me to know today?" The answer that flowed through me changed the trajectory of my life in ways that are still unfolding.

As I put pen to paper, a collection of words poured out—a channeled prayer to help me access the Akashic Records. But why me? That lingering question made me doubt what I inherently knew to be true. I had just been gifted my very own Akashic prayer process.

At the time, I was already teaching others to access their own Records and had developed a certification program that trained aspiring readers to accurately access and provide empowering readings for their clients. I thought to myself, "My current methods are working; why change?"

I assumed that maybe the prayer, later named the Akashic Key Process, was meant only for me. So, I continued to use it in my personal practice for about a year without mentioning this divine gift to anyone.

Then, one day, while hosting a sold-out Virtual Akashic Records Training, I casually mentioned, "I was gifted my own process to access the Records."

I remember it like it was yesterday. A sister-friend and great supporter unmuted herself and asked, "Is that what you're teaching us?" I tried to backpedal, reassuring everyone that the other method was tried and true. But, in the greatest show of faith, the class said, "We don't want to learn the old way. Teach us your new way."

That day, I taught 25 men and women to access the Akashic Records of themselves and others using a process I had only used in my personal practice—and it worked! All 25 participants achieved success, and 10 of those students went on to complete the Practitioner's Certification process.

It is clear that I am a steward. I was given a gift to share as far and wide as I could. I was the chosen conduit to bring this process to humanity. My mission is to help anyone willing to explore the depths of their soul and tap into the infinite wisdom of the Akashic Records. It is a mission that I absolutely love and wouldn't trade for anything.

I hope you enjoy the process of accessing your Akashic Records and feel the peace that comes along with understanding your soul. If you need additional support, please join our Facebook community, Soul Wisdom Akashic, and check out my classes. I offer everything from beginner-level courses to teacher certifications.

Let's embark on this transformative journey together!

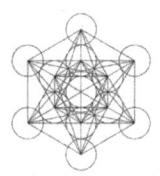

My Why

Most people have an exceedingly profound moment when they find their spiritual path. Mine came about as a natural progression of doing what I loved.

I study dance forms from the African diaspora, primarily Afro-Cuban, Afro-Haitian, and Afro-Brazilian. This exposed me to African Traditional Religions and the cultures where these dance styles originated. I'm highly analytical and had questions. Every answer led to another question and each question-answer combination led me to this wonderful space of metaphysical study and spirituality.

One day, a member of my sister-friend group had an Akashic Record reading and was very excited about it. I wanted to try it for myself.

The reading I received was unlike anything I'd ever encountered.

The reader talked to me about reincarnation, which is something I believed in but never really put much thought into. I'd never delved into what it *actually* meant to live multiple lifetimes. I never speculated about what it meant to truly "return" through each of those lifetimes on a soul level.

She also talked about things I thought were strange and really far out: far-off galaxies, pyramids, and light beings. Some parts deeply resonated with me, so I couldn't write her off. I must admit, though, it stretched what was my current paradigm and got me thinking.

That is when I began to explore the idea of the soul. One thing that stood out to me from one of my session's with her was *soul loss*. I didn't know what it was, but she said I had it. Even in my ignorance, I knew it didn't sound good. Loss indicated that pieces of me were missing, and I was clear I didn't want that. I wanted all my pieces.

I searched to find a solution and had the utmost faith that I would be led to the answer. It was funny because the answer came to me through an email from a list I'd subscribed to for years. I didn't even remember signing up for it and had never even opened any emails. But right there, as I was scrolling through the subject lines in my inbox, the words *soul loss* jumped out at me. There was a class being offered, and I took it.

Not only did I learn how to heal my soul loss, but I learned how to read Akashic Records. During that class, we had to give practice readings, and one practice reading led to another, and then another.

Practice readings led to paying clients and a constant stream of referrals. I booked readings via text messages from my phone. Pretty soon, there were too many inquiries, and I had to create a website. As my business started to grow around readings, clients began to ask me to teach them how to read for themselves. Now, I teach others how to read the Akashic Records, as well as offer a certification for those who want to go deeper and provide services for others.

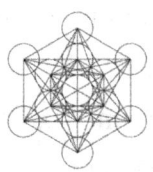

What's Inside

First, I'd like to say you did not find this book by accident and I'm excited to be with you on this journey of learning to read the Akashic Records. You'll identify and clear fears, overcome debilitating patterns, and remove the obstacles that have kept you from moving forward.

In this book, you will find the methods that I teach in my Soul Wisdom Akashic Record courses. You will learn the definition of the Akash and how to read your Akashic Records. I will help you attune to the energy of the Akashic Records. You will learn about the soul and its significance, as well as who you meet when you enter the records.

I encourage you to read this as often as needed to feel comfortable within your Akashic Records. Keep an open mind and know that the information you receive is the guidance you need now. Continue to practice and you will attain additional levels of understanding each time you enter the Akashic Records.

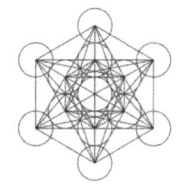

CHAPTER 1

Unveiling the Tapestry of Creation: An Overview of the Akashic Records

"There is no greater gift than the ability to learn yourself by tapping into the highest aspect of yourself." Dr. La Toya Davis

The Soul

Before we delve into the Akashic Records, we need to understand what the soul is. I want to start by saying I firmly believe and teach that multiple truths can exist at the same time. I present information and teach from my truth. As you read the material in the pages to follow, I encourage you to take what resonates and discard what doesn't.

During my first reading, some of the information did not meld with my perception of reality. I had to grow into my understanding. In general, I operate from the position of meeting my clients and my students where they are. So, I encourage you to integrate how you feel in the way you're most comfortable.

At the beginning of creation, there was Source - whatever you perceive Source to be - and all things were Source that existed in and through all that there was. This presented a dilemma. If you're all there is, there's no way you can experience anything else because you are everything. So how could Source experience creation?

In Source's infinite wisdom, it recognized that one way it could experience itself was to break off bits and pieces of itself; an individuation of Source. In that individuation, Source could experience itself. There were many things that were created in this process, including the soul.

I could go down the proverbial rabbit hole with a long and detailed discussion of the soul, but I promise to keep it relevant and bite-sized. The idea of soul individuation means each soul was created to feel, sense, and experience life in a particular way. Source's aim wasn't to experience itself the same way multiple times; it wanted each piece, or individual soul, to have unique experiences. Our literal job as a soul is to explore, play, and create as we live our physical existence. We have been tasked with creating a panoply of experiences for Source to participate in.

Each time we choose to incarnate into a new earthly experience, we also have a choice in how we're going to experience each of these new adventures. We sign on for new lessons that build on lessons of the past. Not just your past within the current incarnation but from past lives as well.

Let's say, for instance, in my previous life I was a rich Baroness and never worked for anything. Everything just came to me. Life was peaceful, and life was great. And then I got bored with that. So when I reviewed my life from the soul level, I said, "Hmm … that was great. I learned a lot, but next time, I want to feel what working to earn money is like. In the next life, I want to experience something like manual labor." This process of selecting, living, learning, and incorporating is constant and happens lifetime after lifetime.

There is a separation and constant connectedness that is consistently at play. We are individuated pieces of Source and fully integrated with Source simultaneously. And for this reason, in the eyes of Source, the Creator, the Universe, God, or whatever term you feel most comfortable using, at soul-level, you are uniquely and perfectly made. Always.

Now, one of the benefits of choosing to be born here on Earth is that we gain the ability to have free will and freedom of choice. This means that even though Source created us to have a particular set of experiences, we are not bound to that. We can choose something else, and we often do. Sometimes we make choices and exercise our free will in ways that go against our nature. When we do this, we create blockages, stress, and strain for ourselves. We can develop ways and habits that keep us stuck in patterns. Essentially, sometimes exercising our free will delays our blessings.

There are a lot of things that can happen when we make choices and have experiences that go against ourselves. Accessing the Akashic Records gives us perspective on the choices we have made that push us out of alignment. We can gain perspective of the choices we've made lifetime after lifetime: all the experiences and the memories. As we continue to come back each time, we don't lose them. They are always a part of us and there for us to access at soul level.

As you access the Akashic Records, hold as your framework that this is a soul-level view; you're getting information with love and without judgment. Because you, as a soul, aren't making mistakes. You are making choices as individuated pieces of Source. There is no judgment, only love. The choices are the choices. We can use the Akashic Records to understand *why* we've made those choices, how those choices are playing out, and if there are any shifts or changes we need to make.

The Akash

The Akash, a Sanskrit term meaning ether, air, or space, holds a profound significance in the realm of spirituality and metaphysics. It is believed to be the fundamental basis and essence of all things in the material world. Often referred to as energy in its earliest state, the Akash represents the point where Source, the primordial essence of existence, manifests its original thought into energy before any action or imprint is made upon it. This sacred moment of creation is where the Akash exists.

Derived from the Akash, the term, "Akashic," signifies the records or repository of knowledge that exists within this energetic realm. When we access the Akashic Records, we venture into the vast energetic space of the Akash. Within this realm, all things are potential and coexist simultaneously. Past, present, and future events intertwine, making it possible for us to pull and receive information from various points in time.

The Akashic Records represent a major energetic field in which every iota of information resides. From the inception of time to all future possibilities, every thought, deed, action, and impulse ever created by every soul is encoded within these vibrational archives. The Akashic Records, a boundless body of consciousness, encompass all existence and are perpetually accessible.

In this chapter, we will embark on a journey through time, exploring the historical context and significance of the Akashic Records in various cultures and spiritual traditions.

The origins of the Akashic Records can be traced back through the annals of history, finding mention in various cultures and spiritual traditions under different names but with consistent themes. One of the earliest references comes from Ancient Egypt, where it was believed that Thoth, the scribe of the gods, maintained a divine library containing records of all events, both past and future. These records, inscribed on golden tablets, were accessible only to those with the necessary spiritual insight, serving as a source of wisdom and guidance.

Ancient Egyptians's belief in an eternal afterlife and the continuity of the soul played a central role in their spiritual beliefs. Rituals and texts guided the soul's journey through the afterlife, preserving memories and experiences from one lifetime to the next.

In Elaine Pagels (1979) *The Gnostic Gospels,* she discusses Gnosticism, an early Christian mystical movement, held the belief in a hidden knowledge, referred to as "gnosis." This divine knowledge was seen as a pathway to understanding one's true nature and connection to the divine.

Some Gnostic texts and teachings suggest a cosmic library of sacred knowledge, akin to the Akashic Records, where seekers could access profound truths about the universe and their place within it. Within this mystical library, seekers could access esoteric teachings and gain insights into the mysteries of existence.

Moving forward, in the late 19th century, the theosophist Helena Blavatsky (1888) brought the concept of the Akashic Records into Western esotericism. Blavatsky described the Akashic Records as a cosmic repository of knowledge, containing the history of the cosmos and the journey of every soul. Her teachings emphasized the interconnectedness of all beings and the existence of a universal consciousness accessible through the Akashic Records.

In the early 20th century, the renowned American psychic Edgar Cayce further popularized the notion of the Akashic Records (Sugrue, 1945). Cayce, often referred to as the "sleeping prophet," claimed to access the

Records in a trance state and provided detailed readings on various topics, including health, past lives, and spiritual growth. His work contributed significantly to the widespread recognition of the Akashic Records as a tool for personal and spiritual development.

Rudolf Steiner, born in the 19th century, was a prominent figure in the development of Anthroposophy, a spiritual philosophy that seeks to bridge the gap between the spiritual and material worlds.

Steiner (1959) introduced the term "Akashic Chronicle" to describe a spiritual record of the events and experiences of humanity and the cosmos. According to Steiner, the Akashic Chronicle could be accessed through spiritual intuition and provided insights into the spiritual evolution of individuals and humanity as a whole.

The term "Akashic Records" itself was coined by Alfred Percy Stinnett (1883) in his book *Esoteric Buddhism*, where he drew upon Eastern spiritual concepts to describe a cosmic storehouse of knowledge. Stinnett's work, influenced by Blavatsky's theosophical teachings, helped popularize the term and concept in Western spiritual circles.

The Akashic Records, known by various names such as the Book of Life in the Bible, or the Akasha, transcend cultural and religious boundaries, representing a universal field of consciousness that encompasses all existence. Whether accessed through meditation, trance, or other spiritual practices, the Akashic Records offer a profound source of wisdom and insight into the nature of reality and the journey of the soul.

Understanding the Akashic Records

The Akashic Records is this major energetic field where we can access all information. Every thought, deed, action, and impulse created from the beginning of time and all future possibilities exist within the Akashic Records. This vibrational body of consciousness exists everywhere in its entirety and is always completely available. The records are an exponential body of knowledge that contains everything that every Soul has ever thought, said, or done over the course of its existence.

You are probably beginning to recognize the limitless information potential within the Akashic Records. However, to keep us on track within the scope of this book, we will focus on the notion of the soul-self and things as they relate to it. So, for our purposes, when discussing the Akashic Records, remember that we are focused on gaining the soul-level view of our choices.

At this point, it is perfectly logical to wonder, can the Akashic Records be used to investigate other people? The short answer is yes, but the more complete response is that you can use the Records to understand yourself in relation to other people or other people in relation to you.

The beauty of the Akashic Records is that because it's a storehouse of every soul's journey, by accessing the records we can truly comprehend how we affect other people and how other people are affecting us. You can't just go in and start gathering information on someone else if it has no direct bearing or relevance to you.

I want to take a moment and really emphasize this because it is not uncommon for us to want to look at things outside of ourselves first. I teach the Akashic Records principle of self evolution.

On a base level, the Akashic Records is a tool for you to understand, heal, and elevate yourself. It is not a place to do harm or a place to go digging around in someone else's business. I would also like to point out that because it contains all future possibilities, it doesn't make for the best source in predicting the future. There are thousands of possibilities that can exist at any given moment in time.

As you continue accessing the Akashic Records, use the information you receive as a frame of reference for how you interact with others and how others interact with you. Use it to heal, grow, evolve, and make changes. I am teaching you to use the records to get the information as it pertains to your soul, unless, of course, you're working with clients who have given you permission to do the work on their behalf.

Ways to Use the Akashic Records

People are drawn to the Records for a multitude of reasons. It is my experience that a lot of people start accessing the records simply because they're curious. Since the Records are known as a good way to access information about past lives, they generally attract a large segment of people who are trying to learn about their own past-life experiences.

Others want the information to aid in healing themselves or searching for a way to be of service to others. The Records allow us to make connections between different events, understand why we are engaging in certain patterns and behaviors, and receive guidance.

In exploring the various ways to use the Akashic Records in your day-to-day life, let's start with the healing aspect. Most people are drawn to the records because something is off. They know that there is something they could do better, a shift that's needed, or some type of change needs to occur. I heard somewhere that you don't find the Akashic Records, they find you. I hold that notion to be true.

Our ability to use the records will allow us to understand what is happening with us and through us, make new choices, and take actions that will enable us to vibrationally heal aspects within ourselves.

We all vibrate at a particular resonance. A simple way to think about this: some days you feel low, and other days you're amped up. Sometimes you meet people and their energy is so great that by being in their presence it takes you to a different time and space. Well, you're responding to their vibrational resonance.

By working in the Akashic Records, you can raise your vibration and find your personal harmonic state. We can use the Records to match the higher resonance, which is more aligned with the experience that our soul intended for us to have before we incarnated.

Use the Records to gain perspective and understand where you're not in alignment. The enlightenment that you can experience from healing within the Akashic Records can bring you abundance, joy, and ease. For instance, in this lifetime, your soul wants to interact with people and be adventurous, and yet you're choosing to live the life of a hermit where you have little to no interaction with people and you rarely do anything outside of your daily routine.

Based on life experiences, it became easier for you to just be alone than deal with people. In the records, you'll be able to see how your past experiences and current choices are preventing you from moving forward and progressing.

Let's look at another example from a client's experience. She was a married woman in her late thirties who had a very successful career and had been clear her whole life she did not want children. In the few years prior to coming to me, she started to entertain the idea of a child but had a lot of fear and reservations about becoming a mother.

Once I opened her Akashic Records, I discovered that three lifetimes ago she had lost a child in a tragic accident and in that lifetime, she blamed herself for her child's death. The records revealed her pain did not end with her in that lifetime, but that she was still carrying the energetic imprint of that past choice today. It was the reason she was unwilling to have children. Using the records allowed us to really look at things in a way to provide understanding, healing, and receive guidance on how to move forward.

It is a soul level view without judgment. This is a modality that you can access any time. It's not like going to a life coach or a therapist. You can receive guidance anytime, day or night. You can ask what choices you can make today to bring yourself in alignment with your goals, what will relieve some of your heartache, and how you can shift the energy in your home? If you're thinking about starting a new job, you can ask what career is in alignment with the path that you've chosen.

Use the records to gain guidance in this lifetime without judgment from a place of love. The possibilities are endless. I use the records for everything; before meetings, before teaching classes, and navigating tough experiences. Why? Because it is a realm of love, it is a realm of light. It has the information and knows the answers.

Instead of struggling through trying to figure out things on your own, explore the endless possibilities that exist by using the Akashic Records. It is said some of the greatest minds have used the Akashic Records to create life-altering inventions and contributions to society by doing the work revealed to them.

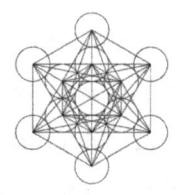

CHAPTER 2

Aligning with the Frequencies of the Universe: The Power of Energetic Attunements

"As energetic beings, we possess the innate capacity to attune ourselves to the rhythms of the universe. Through the power of energetic alignment, we can come into harmonic resonance with the divine frequencies that permeate all of existence, opening ourselves to profound wisdom, healing, and transformation." - Dr. La Toya Davis

Instructions for the Attunement

We are energetic beings accessing an energetic field. The process of the attunement allows us to come into alignment with that particular energetic frequency with greater ease. It is a process by which our energetic field is calibrated to that of the Akashic Records.

For example, think about trying to listen to a particular radio station. The signal broadcasts on a particular frequency which we know as the number we have to find on the radio. Until you land on the correct frequency, you are unable to access the radio station.

Remember driving through towns where you were unfamiliar with the radio stations. Trying to find a radio station that is broadcasting something you want to hear can be challenging, but once you found the station, it was easier to find it again.

That's what the attunement does. It allows you to access the correct frequency with ease because your energy field has already become attuned to the frequency of the Records.

I think of the Akashic Records as a massive house with thousands of rooms that contain multiple access points and doorways. The attunement process makes accessing the Records easier. It allows you to arrive at the right door with the proper key to open it, so you are not standing there fumbling, trying to get in. Further, it gives the most direct path once you get inside.

The attunement process is relatively easy. I have created a short track for you to listen to for five days. Visit, www.learnakashic.com/book, and download the audio file. Find a space where you won't be disturbed, and you can get comfortable. Lay down, stand up, sit down …whatever works for you. Set the intention to become in alignment with the Akashic Records. Listen to the track. Repeat this process for five consecutive days.

I invite you to journal any thoughts, ideas, impressions, or feelings that come up for you each day as you experience the audio and as you move about your day. The best times to listen are before bed or first thing in the morning: First thing in the morning (upon rising) is when we are at our most receptive and directly before bed, we lay the foundation for what our sleep state will experience.

During both of those times, we are less connected to our thinking mind and most connected to the spirit within ourselves. If those times aren't convenient for you, that's perfectly fine. It will work no matter what time of day you listen.

Alternatively, you can skip the attunement process and dive right into accessing the Records. Just remember, this massive house has tons of rooms, so give yourself time to become acclimated, especially if you are new to the experience. Embrace the journey of discovery as you navigate the intricacies of the Akashic Records, seeking profound insights and guidance to enrich your life's path.

I prefer the attunement because it often leads to an easier time — less fog — for the user and makes navigating easier. Just like the information you find in the Records, you choose without fear of judgment or recrimination.

The attunement process serves as the key to the cosmic house of the Akashic Records. By aligning your energetic frequency with the realm of the Akashic Records, you open the doors to profound wisdom and understanding.

Visualize yourself confidently walking through the corridors of this infinite repository of knowledge, ready to explore the countless rooms and access the insights that await. Whether you choose the attunement track or directly embark on your Akashic journey, let this experience be one of self-discovery, healing, and connection to the spiritual truths that guide your soul's evolution. The Akashic Records stand ready to welcome you into their embrace, offering endless possibilities for growth and transformation.

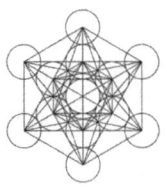

Chapter Notes

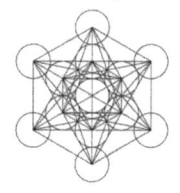

CHAPTER 3

The Cosmic Cast: Understanding the Roles of Energies in the Akashic Records

"In the vastness of our cosmic world, every energy holds a unique purpose and perspective. By recognizing the role each messenger is assigned within the larger landscape, we can better understand and apply the wisdom that is shared with us, ensuring that it aligns with our highest good." - Dr. La Toya Davis

Who We Meet in the Records

Depending on where you are on your spiritual journey, the idea of deities or ancestors or ascended masters may be new to you, or you may be very familiar with the concepts. In my business, I meet people along all variations of the spectrum; I am often asked questions that relate to "who" we talk to while we are in the Records.

Inside the Akashic Records there are the Masters, the Teachers, and the Loved Ones. Keep in mind these are the terms that I use. You may hear other words if you pursue further study; ultimately, you can decide what terms to use. I was first introduced to the concept of the Masters, Teachers, and Loved Ones (MTLOs) in an online course from Linda Howe. In my studies, I have learned other terminology but this is what resonates best and most for me.

Keeper of the Records

At the top level, there is the Keeper of the Records. For me, this energy presents as Archangel Metatron, who in biblical times was the scribe tasked with recording all thoughts, actions, and deeds that had occurred.

This is an oversimplification of Archangel Metatron, but I wanted to provide a relatable reference. The role of the Keeper is to maintain the integrity of the records and monitor and maintain what goes out, who it goes to, how it goes out to them, and when it goes out to them.

The information received from the Akashic Record is not meant to be used to cause harm. It is the job of the Keeper of the Records to maintain the integrity and sanctity of the Akashic field and to prevent access to information that we don't need so that we're not overwhelmed. There can be other Keepers of the Records, but for my teachings, Archangel Metatron is tasked with holding the sacred grid of the Akash. Here is an example of how this can play out:

A former client booked an Intuitive Guidance Session with me during which accessing the Akashic Records isn't necessary. However, during the course of our time together, I realized there was some soul-level information coming to me and it would be more beneficial for me to access her Records. Not even thinking, just acting on impulse, I opened her Record.

I asked the first question and received absolutely no information. I asked another question, and the same thing happened.

I realized I had not gotten her permission to open her records. Once that realization hit me, I asked her permission, and after she agreed, the information started to present itself. That was a moment that I will always remember because it truly showed me how the Record Keepers maintain the integrity of the Records.

Another example is from a client who had a very abusive childhood. She came to me wanting information about her experiences growing up. However, I kept being guided to tell her about an energy modality to help her release some of the emotions tied to her childhood.

She kept asking me about answers to her specific questions and I continued to be guided to the energy modality. Finally, I asked the Records why I couldn't get the answers she wanted.

I was told that she was so angry, anything I offered her in her current state would not bring healing because she could only hear it through the energy of anger. I was given information to help dissipate her anger energy so she would later be in a place to receive the exact answers she wanted.

The Masters

The next level is the Masters. The Masters have never taken physical form. The idea that they never embodied is important because it means that they don't have a point of reference of having lived life and have not had the human experience.

The role of the Master is to maintain and give a perspective from the universal level without emotion and without feeling. The masters show you how you integrate universally with the world at large. Again, because they were with you at your soul's inception, the information spans all lifetimes.

The Teachers

The Teachers are the next level of energy beings that can appear. They show up to give lesson-specific information. Unlike the Masters, the Teachers could have been embodied, so it is possible that they had a human experience.

Examples of Teachers that were embodied would be the Buddha, Mother Mary, and Jesus, to name a few—individuals who came and were highly ascended. The difference between Masters and Teachers is that Masters have a large universal perspective on how our soul fits in. Teachers come in specifically to work with you for a particular lesson or thing.

Loved Ones

Loved Ones will have always been embodied. Loved Ones are people we have met and come into contact with in this existence. They have some type of association with us at the embodied level. A Loved One is not synonymous with an ancestor.

An ancestor can be a Loved One, but the idea of a Loved One is much larger. It could be an elementary school teacher, a spiritual advisor, or anyone significant that you knew. Loved Ones are more inclined to show themselves during a session versus a Master or a Teacher. Sometimes when Loved Ones show up, they will give you some form of identifier so that you know who they are and your connection.

When working in the Akashic Records, we are not working with individual beings or calling on a particular energy to show up. This is where the idea of the Keeper comes in, because the Keeper knows what information we need and who is best to give us that information. So the collective of Masters, Teachers, and Loved Ones come together to provide you with what you need based on what has been passed down by the Record Keeper.

If we use the familiar metaphor of the library to reference the Records, this is how it comes together. Imagine you go to the library and ask for a skydiving book. The head librarian, who is the Record Keeper in this scenario, would then pull out all the books about skydiving. The head librarian asks what specifically you wanted to learn about skydiving and then narrows the books down to the most useful selection and how the library staff (the Masters, Teachers, and Loved Ones) can best share the information with you so it was most relatable.

They work collectively to help you sort through the information so that you have the knowledge you need about skydiving. Without ego or judgment, the team's goal is to deliver the most concise information efficiently and effectively.

Many people ask if they have to do anything such as creating a relationship with these energies while they're in the records. The short answer is no. In order to receive information, you simply show up with a pure mind and a heart open to receive. That's it.

We allow the process and the infinite wisdom of the realm that is the Akash to dictate who we interact with while in the Records. It's not important for us to know who that energy is. It may present itself to you and it may not.

The information that comes to us is always the best information for us at that moment. When we enter the realm of the Akashic Records, it is almost as if you are making an agreement that says "Okay, Keeper of the Records, I trust you to pull the most appropriate information and assign the most appropriate messenger for that information." To become consumed with the details detracts from the larger picture.

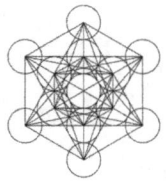

Chapter Notes

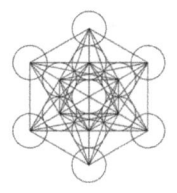

Preparing to Enter the Sacred Realm: Embracing Presence and Releasing Expectations

"The greatest obstacle to success is the preconceived notions we hold. To truly embrace the wisdom of the Akashic Records, we must release our expectations and open ourselves to the authentic experience that awaits us, remaining fully present in the moment." - Dr. La Toya Davis

Key Concepts to Success

When you are in the Akashic Records, there are three key concepts to keep in mind: trust the process, resist doubt, and know this is judgment-free guidance. There's nothing to be afraid of in the Akashic Records. It is a realm of light, and there is no need to fear that some negative energy or entity will give you false information or try to guide you down the wrong path.

Know that if you are in the Records and hear judgments and criticism, that is your ego. The information you receive in the Records is in alignment with you being a divine aspect of Source. You will never have the Records telling you what to do. They won't tell you to leave your job tomorrow, they will only provide you with guidance.

There won't be answers to "Should I … " questions. Those answers you must give yourself and then you will experience one of the infinite possibilities that comes with your choice. You tell the Records what you want and they figure out how to support that.

Your free will and ability to choose for yourself will always be respected. This is the relationship you will have within the Records, and it will grow and build over time. It's like strengthening a muscle. The more you do it, the better and the easier it becomes, like any other relationship.

The realm of the Akashic Records is a place to receive non-judgmental information. All the information that comes through the Akashic Records from the Masters, Teachers, and Loved Ones is there to provide loving guidance.

The aim is to move and progress your soul through this life experience without judgment, which is especially important because we judge ourselves more than anyone else judges us. We think we should have done more; we should have done better. We put all those things on ourselves, but that doesn't take place in the records. The records will always meet you where you are in a very non-judgmental way.

For instance, you know you smoked some weed before entering your records, even though you know it is best to go in with a clear mind. When you enter, there will be no one there saying how dare you smoke weed and then enter the Record. You might only get a little information, but they're not going to judge you for the choice that you made.

Points to Remember

The Records are not a place to escape the realities of life. Unfortunately, some people become so enamored by the energy of the Records and the information they receive, they spend excessive amounts of time in the Akashic Records for escape. We want to stay grounded in our 3D realm and recognize the Records are a tool to help us move through this reality, not escape from it.

There are two aspects to the information you will receive in the Akashic Records. First, there's the fixed aspect, which is our blueprint, and it doesn't shift. If you ask the same question today or 30 years from now, it will still be the same answer. Second, there's the evolving aspect; those things shift according to our choices. Where do you live? Did you go to college? Did you have one child or two? What career did you take? Those are evolving aspects.

You don't have to be psychic to go into your Akashic Records. Often people are intimidated by their lack of experience with doing anything even remotely similar. The reality is that we all can connect with information beyond our physical perception. The Records are accessible to anyone willing to learn the process and put in the effort.

It's not an out-of-body experience. You don't have to go into a trance. You want to be fully present with yourself the whole time you're in the records.

Intent is especially important. You must be clear on your intention when asking questions within the records. Even if your intention is just to relax and receive some good energy, you must be clear on it.

Remember, don't try to predict the future.

The question always determines the answer. The Akashic Record will never give you an answer to a question you didn't ask. This is about guidance, not telling you what to do or judging you.

So, if you were to ask a question such as showing you the relationship that you had with your daughter in previous lifetimes, then that is the answer you would receive. Not your relationship with your aunts or uncles. It would show you that maybe you were siblings at one point in time, friends at another. It's not going to take you to her birth, because that moment is not about your relationship. So, the answer is always going to be determined by the question.

Be mindful that everybody's experience in the records is different. Therefore, you cannot judge your experience based on someone else's experience.

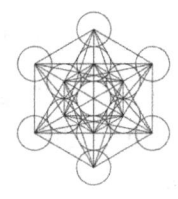

CHAPTER 5

Deciphering the Language of the Soul: Understanding Your Claires

"Having a Claire ability is not a superpower. We all possess these innate gifts. The true superpower lies in recognizing and embracing this universal truth."
- Dr. La Toya Davis

Ways to Receive Information

We all naturally possess Claires, or innate gifts, through which we access spiritual wisdom and insight. Claires are the way the Akashic Records provide us with the information we need. Each person comes to this work with a different level of development. However, one thing is true, EVERYONE has access to a Claire.

Let's take a quick look at the main ways you can receive information while in the Records…

Clairaudience, or clear hearing, is akin to receiving a whispered secret from the universe. Imagine an invisible friend who speaks in a voice only you can hear, offering guidance, insights, or sometimes, just comfort. This ability can manifest as external or internal sounds, music, or words that resonate with a deeper truth or message. As you attune your listening, both internally and externally, you cultivate this gift, learning to distinguish these divine communications from everyday noise.

Clairvoyance, or clear seeing, is like having an inner eye that glimpses beyond the tangible, into the realms of possibility and truth. It might manifest as vivid dreams, symbols, or flashes of insight that appear unexpectedly, providing guidance or affirmation. This is my secondary claire, and it primarily shows up while doing work in the Akashic Records. To enhance clairvoyance, visualizing and trusting in the images that come to you can be powerful, as these are often messages from your higher self or the Akashic Records.

Clairalience, or clear smelling, involves intuitive recognition through scent, connecting us to memories, feelings, or even spiritual presences. Like an unexpected breeze carrying a familiar fragrance, this sense can evoke profound connections to past experiences or loved ones. Cultivating clairalience involves paying attention to the scents hat permeate your experiences, recognizing when they might carry a message or significance beyond their physical source.

Clairgustance, or clear tasting, is perhaps the most enigmatic of the Claires. It offers intuitive insight through taste sensations unrelated to physical eating. Imagine savoring a flavor that suddenly, inexplicably appears, carrying a message or memory. For example, your mouth suddenly tastes like a cigar. You haven't smoked anything, but you can taste cigar smoke in your mouth. This sense might connect you to a specific person, place, or emotion, serving as a subtle yet profound form of guidance or connection.

Clairsentience, or clear feeling, is an intuitive awareness experienced through physical sensations or emotions. It's like having an internal compass that offers direction through feelings, rather than words or visuals. This sense can guide you towards or away from people, situations, or decisions, based on the sensations of harmony or discomfort you experience. This is what people mean when they say they have a gut feeling. Clairsentience is the knowledge you receive when your gut tells you to do or not do something. Honing clairsentience involves listening to these bodily signals, recognizing them as messages.

Claircognizance, or clear knowing, stands out as the intuitive voice of certainty within us. It is a sudden understanding or insight, unattached to logic or reasoning, that arrives with clarity and conviction. My primary claire is Claircognizance. I describe it as a thought suddenly flashing in my mind and I know it to be true just as surely as I know my name. It doesn't matter what I'm doing, I could be in the middle of a conversation and then it's just there. I didn't ask about it. It just downloads into my head, whatever it is, with a very clear knowing. And the reason it's difficult for people to believe is because it does just pop into your head. You think it's just a random thought, not purposely given from the Universe. To cultivate claircognizance, embracing moments of spontaneous insight and trusting in their validity can affirm and strengthen this connection.

Clairempathy deals with intuitive emotion, enabling us to feel and understand the emotional states of others deeply. It's a heart-centered knowing that can foster profound connections and empathy. This claire requires the establishment of boundaries to maintain your emotional well-being. Learning to discern your own emotions from those of others and creating protective energetic practices are crucial steps for those with clairempathy. This can ensure that your gift serves as a bridge to understanding, rather than a source of overwhelm.

Continued work in the Akashic Records develops your claires over time as well. I mentioned clairvoyance is my secondary claire. Well, now it is a sense I rely on frequently and can receive a great deal of information from. However, prior to my work in the Records, it was an undeveloped spiritual gift. I had access to it but without consistency. This strengthening of other claires is a common occurrence while working in the Records.

Considerations About Receiving information

Comparison is a thief of joy. Your experience in the records is your experience. I often notice when teaching live courses that when someone shares an experience, if another person doesn't feel like it matches up to theirs, they think that something is wrong—forgetting that the information came to them in a way that was exactly right for them.

If you sit and get the proverbial crickets, then troubleshooting is necessary. Whenever that happens, I ask questions, probing into the experience, usually you will find there was actually more happening than you were aware of.

A good place to start with troubleshooting questions if you do not believe you are receiving any information through one of the Claires. Ask yourself, in this moment:

- What do I feel?
- What do I see?
- What do I hear?

- What do I sense?
- What do I know?
- What do I smell?
- What do I taste?

Just remember, your experience doesn't need to be like anyone else's. Don't put too much pressure on yourself. Just be open, go with the flow, trust the process. Let go of any preconceived expectations. You miss out on parts of your message when you hold on to how you thought the experience was going to be. Let all of that go.

As a matter of fact, before we move into the grounded meditation that follows, I want you to take a moment and actively release any expectation you have about how you are going to receive information. When I am not in the Records, I have a very difficult time utilizing my gift of clairvoyance. While in the Records, though, my natural gift of claircognizance is diminished and clairvoyance is enhanced. You just never know, and I want you to be ready and open for that type of experience.

Here is an affirmation you can say to clear any mind debris. *I am open to receive information in a multitude of ways.* Repeat this whenever you start to doubt your ability to receive clear information.

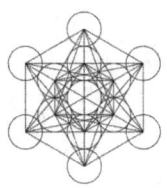

Chapter Notes

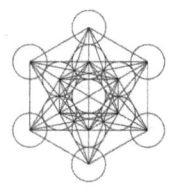

CHAPTER 6

Grounding in the Present Moment: A Meditation for Accessing the Akashic Records

"Grounding is simply a conscious act of slowing down, connecting with ourselves, and becoming one with the earth beneath our feet." - Dr. La Toya Davis

Grounded Meditation

We are going to do a grounded meditation. To get the most out of it, either read the following instructions before you begin or read each paragraph and pause to experience each stage of the meditation. You can also record yourself reading the meditation and play it as you go through the exercise or visit www.learnakashic.com/book and download the audio recording.

I want you to get comfortable wherever you are. Sitting or lying down. Whatever feels most comfortable for you. I want you to hold an intention for this meditation for your time here and for your time moving forward, as we continue to work and learn the process of using the Akashic records.

As you set that intention, I just want you to take intentional breaths, breathing in through the nose, and out through the mouth. Become aware of your breath each time you do it. Continue to breathe in through the nose and breathe out through the mouth. Just notice the breath; that's all you're doing.

This time, as you breathe in through the nose, I want you to breathe in that intention that you set for yourself. I want you to breathe out anything that is counter to your ability to achieve that intention. Let's do those two more times. Breathe in your intention and breathe out anything that does not support that intention.

Last one. Breathe in that intention. See, feel, sense, or know that breath moves from the top of your head all the way to the bottom of your feet. Release anything that does not serve that intention.

As you become aware of your breath and your space, I want you to notice the top of your head. You don't have to make any judgment about anything, just start at the top of your head and start to bring your attention downward. As you move from the top of your head, through your eyes, through your nose, through your mouth, you release any tension, any frustration, anything that you're holding on to.

Continue scanning through the throat, through the heart, through the chest, just letting go. Continue to breathe into all areas of the body, through the stomach, through the pelvis, continuing to breathe and release. No judgment. Just breathe and release through the legs, through the knees, all the way down to the feet.

When you get to your feet, just take one big breath, and send all of the energy through the feet. As you send that energy through your feet, it travels down into the Earth. As that energy travels down into the Earth, the earth creates anchoring cords with all that you set down. And in its infinite wisdom, it knows the parts that need to be anchored and it knows the parts that need to be released and transmuted into something else.

Continue to breathe from the top of the head, sending that energy down through the bottom of the feet. Release all things that do not serve you. Hold the intention for all the things that you want and need. Just continue to see that cycle. From the top of the head through the feet knowing, sensing, feeling, and believing that the Earth is infinite in its wisdom to ground you in a way beyond anything that we can imagine.

As you continue breathing, those grounding cords get stronger. They anchor you firmly into the core of the Earth. As this cord locks in the center of the Earth, the Earth agrees to accept anything you release. What you let go cannot return to you in the same capacity that it was released, but can be transmuted into an energy that you can use for your growth and elevation. Know your intention is set and breathe that knowing back through your body.

Now you're going to go in the opposite direction. Know that the state of being grounded, that support and stability we just created, is coming back through the feet, through the legs, through the knees, through the top of the thighs, into the pelvis, through the stomach, into the chest, through the heart, through the throat, the mouth, the eyes to the top and crown of the head. This knowing, this support, this stability is extending straight up above the head. As far as your mind's eye can see or go.

As this energy extends up and over your head, it turns into a very bright white light that is the epitome of love, support, compassion, healing, and forgiveness. This white light is nurturing, supportive, and it funnels into you in whichever way you need it most. You see, sense, feel, or know this to be true as this white light continues to encapsulate you and fill you with love, compassion, forgiveness, and hope.

This white light is feeding your intention and growing your intention; it's amplifying and activating every part of you that is in support of your intention. You already have all that you need. And this white light activates all aspects of you that were asleep, that were dormant, that were shut off, that were disconnected, that prevented you or that will prevent you from accessing your abilities to move forward working in the Akashic Record, and moving forward and accessing your intuition.

This white light has canceled all that. You are in complete alignment with your intention. You are in complete alignment with love energy, you are in complete alignment with Source as the Divine Being and standing within your soul's energy.

With this knowledge, take this white light; feel it, see it, sense it, and just breathe in from the top of the head all the way down to the bottom of the feet. Feel it cover you 360 degrees. The intention that we set today is active across all dimensions of space and time and throughout all portals.

Know this to be true, and take a few more deep breaths to release anything that you may have forgotten before but is coming up now. Set any additional intention that you didn't think of before but is coming up now. Know that the Earth is smart enough to know what needs to be released and what needs to be planted, that Source through this white light is smart enough to know what needs to be amplified and what needs to be canceled.

Breathe out whatever you need to. Know this intention has been set. Take your final, deep breath. Know all things to be true. I want you to say out loud, "And so it is." Drop your chin to your chest when you're ready to bring yourself back into active space. Open your eyes when you're ready and grab a drink of water to fully ground yourself back into your space.

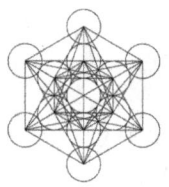

Chapter Notes

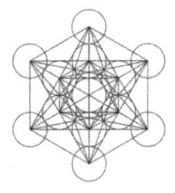

CHAPTER 7

Crossing the Threshold: The Art of Opening and Closing the Akashic Records

"I live my life in such a way that my actions become my prayers. Through this conscious approach, I am in a constant state of prayer." - Dr. La Toya Davis

Opening and Closing the Records

A t this point you should be grounded, centered, believing in yourself, and ready to open the Akashic Records.

You've had an overview of what the Akashic Records are, different ways to use them and we've talked about some key considerations to keep in mind as you're working through the process. As I introduce opening the Records, what I want you to keep in mind is that we are not diving deep, we're just dipping our toe in the water while accessing the records.

This is about becoming comfortable with accessing your own records; that's it. I emphasize viewing this as a method for accessing your own records because the approach to opening the records for others differs and involves extra factors.

The process that you're going to use is the Akashic Key Process, which is really a prayer. The Masters, Teachers and Loved Ones in 2019 gifted me this process, and I have been exclusively teaching it and certifying others to use it since 2020.

For more in-depth study about navigating your personal records, or learning how to access the records of others and become certified, consider checking out my self-paced Akashic Records courses or live training modules found at www.chicourses.com.

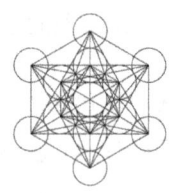

Akashic Key Process –
Opening Prayer

I give thanks to the Masters, Teachers, Loved Ones, and Keepers of the Akashic Record for preserving the sanctity of the Akashic field.

At this time, I intend to enter into my Akashic Records.

With a clear mind and a pure heart, I come to receive information in alignment with achieving my highest good on this plane and my soul's journey.

Remove from me any self-centeredness or remnants of ego that would cause conflict with receiving information in the light of love from which it flows.

Attune me instantly to the highest vibration for clarity, love, light, and elevation.

Thank you, Thank you, Thank you.

The Records are now open.

R ead this prayer each time you go into your Akashic Records. Think of your time in the records as a conversation where you will be asking for things. The prayer is the conversation starter. Let's examine the prayer line by line.

We come into the Records with an air of gratitude and of thanksgiving through the opening statement. Next, we set our intention. Remember we're looking for answers and the records meet you where you are, so you need to be in a space to receive.

The third line follows suit but expands into saying that you're coming with a clear mind and a pure heart. Most importantly, you're coming to receive information in alignment with your highest good. That statement removes the gray area of what you think is best for you and opens you up to the universal greatness that is there. You are now open to your highest good on this planet and the highest good for your soul's journey.

We follow this by how you are going to function in the Records. Oftentimes, the biggest issue people have in receiving information in the records is the ego. Although the ego simply does its job, it may jump in sometimes when we're in the Records. So, this particular statement is about showing up open to receive information and your awareness of the need to remove the parts of ego or the things that are self-centered.

We can sometimes hear something we don't want to that causes conflict within ourselves and impedes us from receiving information. When we say the fourth sentence of the prayer, it instantly sends us into the proper vibration, to be in alignment with whatever thing we need to receive in that moment.

You end by giving thanks, completing the prayer to open the Records.

One of the things I want you to focus on as you enter the Records is that energy follows intent. Mentally, your mind understands these words, and it's okay if you aren't sure of the nuisances at an intellectual level. The prayer sets the intention and the energy will follow.

Know that with this prayer, you enter into a process. It works on the spiritual plane by giving the thinking mind something to anchor into. Although there are multiple ways to enter into the Records, the Akashic Key Process gives the mind a very concrete way of knowing this is happening. By saying it aloud, we are allowing the intention to be set firmly across all dimensions of space and time.

Now read over it a few times until you feel it truly resonates within you. After you've done so, journal about anything that comes up for you.

Akashic Key Process – Closing Prayer

Every time you open the Records you must close them. To close the Akashic Records we have another simple prayer:

Thank you to the Masters, Teachers, Loved Ones, and Keepers of the Akashic Record for sharing wisdom and energy with me today. As I close my records, may the energetic exchange of healing and guidance continue to resonate.

Thank you, Thank you, Thank you.

The Records are Now Closed.

Notice how it's basically the same structure. We start with giving thanks.

Think about when you are done hanging out with someone who has helped you and it's time to say your goodbyes. Typically, you say, "Thank you."

That's the first statement, acknowledging what they've done and showing gratitude. You then set your intention to close the Records.

Not only are you closing your Record, but you want this exchange of healing and guidance to continue. Then we thank them again and declare the records are now closed. By doing so we sever the connection between us and the energetic field that is the Akash.

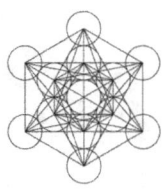

Chapter Notes

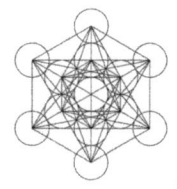

CHAPTER 8

Navigating the Labyrinth of Wisdom: The Power of Effective Questioning

"The question we ask will always determine the answer we receive. Since we cannot change this fundamental principle, let us focus our energy on asking better questions." - Dr. La Toya Davis

Phrasing Questions

To gain access to your Records, you have to ask questions. Up to this point, you have gone through the Attunement process, you've become acclimated to the records, you've tested the energy to see what it felt like, and now we are going to explore how to get information and move through the records. There are three major rules when it comes to asking questions:

1. Avoid questions centering around time and when things will happen. The Records are full of all future possibilities, which means there are an innumerable number of choices that could alter a projected timeline. There are also factors outside of our control such as other people's contributions and choices.

   To answer time-and-when questions, you would have to navigate and scan the entire realm of possibilities of "if this, then that". The Akashic records are not an ideal tool for prediction.

   You can ask in a way to get a sort of estimate based on your current path. You could include the phrase, "... giving all things remaining the same…", and you would gain your answer based on that. But, shifts happen every day and tomorrow you can decide on an action that completely puts a monkey wrench in everything that you were doing.

   Your trajectory is going to shift as well, and that will alter some of the answers. Remember, the records give you answers based on where you are right now and take into account the journey you're taking.

   Also, time as we know it is not the same in the Akashic Records. Within the Records, all things are happening at the same time, so the ability to get a sense of what's happening when and how is a bit jaded. So, again, avoid asking time-and-when questions.

2. The next rule is a major one for me. As a self-empowerment coach, my purpose is to get people to stand in their power and to honor and be accountable to themselves and for themselves. With that being said, "Should I," questions are a way to abdicate responsibility for choice. It's a way to get someone else's opinion, or in this case, an energetic interjection about what they think we should do. That is not what the records are for.

   Instead, the Records provide guidance for you at the soul level; it is not to tell you what to do. If you receive information, and it has this sense of telling you what you should do or what you better not do, then you must check your ego. Only loving guidance comes from the Records.

   Asking questions like, "Should I marry Sam," or "Should I take this job," releases your responsibility and gives it over to someone else. This is the opposite of how we want to use the Records. The whole purpose of going into the Akashic Records is about getting information and guidance to help us navigate choices in our lives.

3. Avoid yes-or-no questions. Asking questions such as, "Will I be able to go on a trip to Egypt," or, "Will I benefit from getting out of the house today," should not be your primary method of questioning. Asking yes-or-no questions for clarity while in the Records is okay, but asking yes-or-no questions as the only way of questioning will not provide the depth that is available within the Records. Let me give you an example.

   Let's say you asked, "Will I be able to go on a trip this weekend with my friends?" The Record says yes, and you think everything will be good. You take the trip and end up getting into an argument with one of your companions. As a result, your housing is messed up, and your flights are rescheduled. It is just one thing after another, and you're confused because you believe the Records said, "Yes."

Often when you have a yes-or-no question as your primary inquiry, it would be beneficial to dig deeper into your true intention so you can reframe your question to be more beneficial and in alignment with what you truly desire. If your intention is to party, you can ask:

- Will I have a good time if I go on this trip this weekend?
- What are some benefits of going on the trip this weekend?
- What are possible challenges for going on the trip?
- Are there lessons waiting for me if I go on this trip? If so, what are they?

You want to phrase the questions in a way that will give you depth of information so that you can make informed decisions. The other thing about yes-or-no questions, depending on the question, is they can act as just another way for us to abdicate our responsibility.

The same thing goes for working with clients if you choose to do so. You will frequently have someone in a session asking should I do this, can I do this, and you will want to encourage them to think a bit deeper about what it is that they're actually trying to do.

Let's go back to the should-I-marry-Sam question. By delving deeper into the energy behind the question, we can reframe it.

To further explore the energy behind the inquiry, I would ask the client what they want to happen if they marry Sam. If the client says they want to be happy and feel supported, a stable financial situation, and to feel passion, I have a better understanding of the energy they seek. I would reframe the question from should they marry Sam into something more along the lines of showing if marriage to Sam leads to happiness and passion, feeling supported, and financial stability. I would ask what lessons will they work through together, challenges that may arise, and what will the client learn on their own?

In addition to the three major rules for asking questions within the Akashic Record, feel free to explore and find what ways work best for you. Be sure to write down the questions that you ask as well as the answers that you receive and how you receive them.

This last step is especially important because looking at your questions and the answers you received is a wonderful learning tool. You ascertain the nuances around the different ways to ask questions and receive information. This enables you to recognize how to adjust your phrasing.

Before I end this chapter, let me touch briefly on yes-or-no questions again. I don't want you thinking you can't ask any yes-or-no questions because they're unavoidable, but they should only be asked for clarity. Questions such as, "Are there any lessons for me to learn here?" That's a yes-or-no question, but it leads you to the next question of asking the Records to show you the lessons. Keep in mind, if you ask a question and you don't feel you've received any more information about the situation than when you started, go back and rethink how to ask the question, what your true intention is, and what the energy of the inquiry is.

*Note: These are general rules. As with all things, the more you become familiar with something, your ability to navigate it grows. The Akashic Records are the same.

Asking Questions is Like a Conversation

I want you to recall that when we opened Akashic Records, I stated it was like the beginning of a conversation. I want you to continue with that theme while you're asking questions within the Records. Think of it as having a conversation with someone that loves you and wants the best for you no matter who you are or what you've done. You receive information from them with ultimate and complete love. Within a conversation, you ask questions and you receive information, then you ask another question and receive some more information, and you continue with this exchange of information and follow-up questions.

One of my favorite examples is based on asking a standard question. Let's suppose while in the Records I asked, "What is something that would be beneficial for me today?" If the answer was to go outside in the sun, the conversation could continue like this:

- Why is going in the sun beneficial for me?
  o Your energy is low, and the sun will help you recharge your energy.
- Are there other ways or things I could do to get energy?
  o Yes, you could drink some water because you're dehydrated, and your cells aren't functioning well.

That's the type of conversation you want to have within the Records. If you receive an answer that's not very clear, ask for more information. It's okay to say that you don't understand and that it's not clear. It's okay to ask them to show you in another way or in a specific way that will make it clear for you. That's perfectly fine; the Masters, Teachers and Loved Ones are learning and gaining an understanding about what works best for you. Think of approaching the questions with child-like curiosity.

In one of my live courses, I had a student who said everything was just spinning during their attunement process. During the class, we went into an Akashic reading session, and she said everything was still spinning, so I asked her if she told it to slow down.

I use this as an example because this is not a rigid process. These are not authority figures that you just have to go with whatever it is and have no other options. This is a loving relationship. When she next went into the Records, she asked for the spinning to slow down and it did. It was nothing but her energy adjusting to be within the field.

Remember at all times you maintain your divine authority so you never need to be afraid to ask for what you need.

Assignment

You now have all the tools you need to go into your Records and receive information effectively. I want you to take some time each day, maybe three to five minutes, and I want you to go through the process of opening and closing your records. While you're in your Record, all I want you to do is hold the intention of becoming acclimated to the realm or the energetic vibration of the Akashic Records.

A simple question that you can ask during this week is what you need to do each day. During this acclimation process, you will be exploring how you receive information through your different claires. You explore how you naturally receive information. Is it through feeling, sight, sound, knowing, smell or taste? Or is it a combination?

During this time, it will be necessary to first become aware and then accustomed to the small ways you receive information such as flashes of color or random sounds. Keep record of them.

This is what your practice process could look like:

Open your records, ask your question and follow-up questions, make notes of whatever comes up for you and how it came up for you. Did you see it, smell it, hear it, know it, or taste it? Write it down and anything that went along with it. Then, as you go throughout your day, make mental note of everything that even remotely seems associated with your session. You can also put that in your journal.

This will enable you to see and tie certain things together. If you reach a point that you want to ask different questions, feel free to change the questions. The question I provided is just a sample question I use in my daily life. You will find a list of additional questions available in the Appendix.

The last thing that I want to point out is that once you set your intention and enter into the Records, you need to trust whatever comes up for you. Expect the intentions set in the Akashic process to hold true. Remember, the intention wasn't just to enter and receive information from the realm of the Akash; it was also to put the ego and self-centeredness aside. Those were the intentions that you set, so in this moment you trust, know, and believe that you are in alignment with that intention and whatever comes to you is exactly what you need in that moment.

Asking Questions to Resolve Issues

The amount of information available while in the Akashic Records can be overwhelming. For this reason, I like to use the *Blockage Resolution Protocol*, a structured way to work while in the Records. This structure is useful if you want some type of resolution or healing by working through a particular problem.

First, you need to complete the pre-work of the Blockage Resolution Protocol by really understanding the current situation. If every year I have to buy a car because my car always stops working for one reason or another, there's something here that needs to be explored beyond faulty cars.

Identify the outcome you want such as buying a car in good working order. Why do I want that? I want the security and stability of knowing that I have reliable transportation without the frustration of buying a new car every year.

Journal, get your thoughts together, drill down to your true intentions and what you really need from the situation. When the pre-work is done, you go into the Records. You now know your intent, and we're going to ask questions in a systematic way that will allow you to get to the next steps.

When you're in the Records, you can identify the root cause of the situation: Why do you buy cars that only last a year? Digging into the root cause leads to discovering what you may need to release followed by the action you need to take.

Following the car example, maybe you know you need to buy better cars, but you don't feel like you deserve a nicer car. This realization can lead to you understanding that you do deserve a nice (and reliable) vehicle.

Who do you need to become to achieve this? Some of the actions you could take include renting a nice car or taking a luxury vehicle for a test drive to start opening yourself to the experience. Maybe there's a financial block at play, so your action step would be to save the equivalent of three car payments before you buy anything.

That was an example of what the process would look like. Reference the Appendix to see the full protocol.

Everything I offer can be customized to what feels and works best for you. When looking at the protocol sheet, pay special attention to the structure of the sentences because by now, you know the question determines the answer. You can get incomplete answers because you've asked poorly phrased questions.

The way questions are worded on the protocol sheet and on the Essential Resource question list, will really help you get to the crux of the matter. Moving through things in this way helps remove some of the ambiguity from the process. There are thousands of questions that you can ask. Look through how the questions are structured, and the categories will really give you a clear understanding of how this works.

Cleaning Up Questions

I want to take this chapter to go deeper into moving through the questions.

You may ask a question in the Records and not get an answer. That could occur because the Keeper doesn't believe you are ready for the answer or because of the way you phrased your question.

For instance, if you ask, "What is my true life purpose?" and receive silence, try this instead: "Am I ready to understand my true life purpose at this moment?" This phrasing can clarify whether the silence is a response itself or a cue to refine your query.

Another strategy you can use is to break down a question into smaller pieces or expand it to prompt a response and gain clarity about why you didn't get an answer the first time you asked. Imagine you ask, "Why am I facing challenges in my relationship?" and receive no response. You could narrow it down to, "What aspect of my behavior contributes to these relationship challenges?" You could also broaden this into, "What lessons am I to learn from my current life experiences?"

This rephrasing can unveil new layers of insight or redirect your focus to a more productive area of inquiry. Suppose your question, "Why can't I find fulfillment in my job?" is met with silence. Consider dissecting this broad inquiry to pinpoint potential blockages. You might ask, "Is there a specific belief hindering my job satisfaction?" By isolating aspects of your broader question, you can unearth underlying issues and gain clarity on why the initial answer was obscured.

Also, make sure you don't ask multiple questions in one question. Ask only one question at a time. An example question would be, "How would I benefit from moving to Kansas City and starting this new job?" That might seem like one question but it's actually two; moving to Kansas City and starting a new job. Each will have its own impact on what you're trying to do—advance your career and the role moving to Kansas City will have on the rest of your life.

The wording of the original question will skew how the information comes to you. Keep the questions separate to foster clearer, more actionable responses from the Records.

One more, very important thing about asking better questions is making sure that you are detached from the answer. Sometimes we can ask questions in a way that can prejudice the outcome. Be mindful about spending time in the Records as your opportunity to get information and guidance in a non-judgmental way.

Enjoy the freedom to explore without attachment, from a place of wanting to know so that you can grow, learn and understand instead of trying to manipulate the questions so they lead to a specific answer. Your objective is not to create limitations with your questioning but be completely open and free.

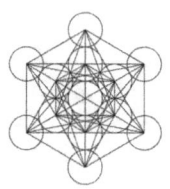

Chapter Notes

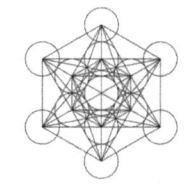

CHAPTER 9

Transmuting Energy for Transformation: Clearing and Resetting in the Akashic Records

"The Law of Physics states that energy can neither be created nor destroyed, but we possess the power to transmute it for our highest good and greatest benefit at all times." - Dr. La Toya Davis

Understanding Clearing and Resetting

Before we discuss how to go about clearing the Akashic Records, I want you to understand that although I'm giving you certain processes, you can simply just ask while you're in the Records. When working in the Akashic Records it is important for you to lean into your own intuition. Ask the Masters, Teachers, and Loved Ones what you can do, or try some of the processes, tips, and suggestions I give you. Always trust what comes up for you.

So, what do I mean about clearing the Akashic Records? At this point, you understand that we have the ability to access all things past, present, and future while in the Akashic Records. The reason being, of course, is that in the realm of the Records, time is flat. All things are happening at the same time: past, present, and future.

It is also important to note that clearing and resetting both occur while you are in the Records.

In our 3D realm, things happen now, and we have the records (individual and collective history) of the past and a concept of the future. When we clear the Akashic Records, we are shifting, disturbing, and dismantling energetic patterns. That's important because in our present moment, these energetic patterns and frequencies are with us.

They vibrate and resonate towards particular things, and as long as those frequencies continue to resonate or send out a particular signal, we attract what matches a particular vibration. Think of it as an energetic beacon, and as long as that energetic beacon is broadcasting at that particular energetic frequency, we receive things in resonance with the specific frequency.

When we clear and heal through the Records, we work to shift and change the energetic vibration attached to certain memories, triggers, or trauma. Whatever that thing is, our plan is to no longer send out the same frequency. When we disrupt that energy, we disrupt the energetic pattern.

When we clear in the Akashic Records, we need to make sure what we disrupt is replaced with something that shifts, changes, and/or raises our frequency for greater alignment with what we want to attract. That, in essence, is what I'm referring to when I talk about clearing and resetting in the Akashic Records.

We're not going back and changing actual events. The event was the event; it happened. Instead, what we're doing with a particular record is understanding the energetic imprint and pattern so that we can change the energy of the beacon and what resonates with us.

Clearing With Words

Alright, let's break it down into simple terms—clearing and resetting within the Akashic Records is surprisingly straightforward when you grasp the core concept: energy follows intention. The first crucial step? Pinpointing the issue - like an agreement you unconsciously made in your youth and still follow - and recognizing how it's manifesting in your life today. Awareness is key here; you must shine a light on those hidden corners to start the clearing process.

Let's use the job opportunity in Kansas as an example. While in the Records, you stumble upon a belief that's capping your income potential. During the clearing, you'd assert, "I cancel this limiting belief across all dimensions of space and time." But it's not just about saying it; it's about embedding this new narrative into your consciousness and taking new action based on your newfound awareness.

When we talk about clearing, imagine you're tidying up not just any space, but a multi-dimensional one. You start the cleanup in the Akashic Records—that's on the fifth floor. Then, we bring that clarity down to the fourth floor to our thoughts and our awareness. Finally, that trickles down to the third floor, which is the realm where you move and take action everyday. Think of it as aligning our upstairs with our downstairs, ensuring our entire being is on the same page.

Take this scenario: You run every time you spot a dog, but you don't understand why because, hey, you've never had a bad dog encounter with a dog in this life. You dive into the Akashic Records, and you uncover a past-life trauma with a dog. You set the intention to clear this energy, and you state, "I clear the energetic imprint of this memory across all dimensions of space and time."

Now you understand. You've got context, and that shifts everything. Instead of an autopilot reaction, you have a choice. Your fifth floor (realm of the Akashic Record) awareness allows for the clearing by reciting the statement, which triggers an automatic new thought on the fourth floor each time you now see a dog. At the level of action (third floor) you can make a new choice without the energetic prompting of the old imprint. That's the power of awareness.

But remember, clearing isn't just about chanting a magical statement in the Records. It's about change—actual, tangible change in how you act, think, and respond. If you clear a pattern in the fifth dimension but keep replaying the old tapes in the third, guess what? You're back to square one.

Clearing With Images

Another method I use for clearing is called the progression method—perfect for those who use visualization or can create a sense of knowing within their mind's eye. This method calls on you to see yourself from a state of lack to a place of thriving in a logical fashion.

The process leading up to clearing is the same. You go into the Records, you identify a blockage, and now you progress to the happy resolution.

To illustrate this, let's talk about Naomi. Naomi is completely destitute, her car has been repossessed, she's been evicted, and she has barely enough clothes to get through the week. Naomi can't imagine herself with $100,000 in the bank and her life overflowing with abundance in all its forms.

With the progression method, Naomi creates a story for the Akashic Record. She could visualize it, write it, sing it, dance it, whatever feels most natural. No matter how she does it, she must do it within the Record.

In this scenario, a past life vision in the Records shows Naomi giving her life to the church; her car, the deed to her house, all her clothes, everything. This is when the vow of poverty was created. As Naomi sees this happening, she says, "I cancel this vow of poverty across all dimensions of space and time. I intend this vow to be inactive now."

Now that she has awareness, Naomi moves into the stage of clearing and resetting. Her visualization could include seeing herself walking to the clergy and tearing up a piece of paper that looks like it has her signature on it.

This is the list of all the things that she has given. Naomi tears it up, canceling it by ripping it to shreds and throwing it in the garbage.

Naomi walks away, and removes all of her clothes from the closet and puts them in a bag. Next, she walks into an office to get her car keys. Naomi walks out the door, gets in her car, and feels so good because she doesn't have to worry about having to ask anybody to take her anywhere. We progress to Naomi walking into a bank where she deposits money so she can use her debit card.

As you can see, Naomi went from a low point to a middle point. She's not at $100,000 in the bank because that's too much outside of Naomi's capacity right now, but she's in a place that is much better. She physically severed the connection with a scarcity mindset and took action all while she was inside the Record.

The example of Naomi is an example of clearing and resetting because she replaced old energy that doesn't serve her with beneficial energetic vibration so new choices can be made.

Through this gradual narrative, Naomi isn't just making symbolic gestures; she's rewriting her energetic script. We're not catapulting her into a fantasy but guiding her to a sustainable, improved state, where she's actively choosing her new path.

When working within the Akashic Records, you must not think of it as a magic pill. Saying the clearing statement in the Records is only part of the process.

New behaviors and new patterns are what make things happen and bring the progression to a conclusion. When you clear it energetically in the Akashic Record, that energetic beacon doesn't go out anymore. If we don't change our behavior and our reactions or the way we think about the issue, then we'll just replace the beacon with something similar and it will begin to broadcast again.

Let's look at another example of a blockage you can find while in the Records. Imagine while investigating if you should take the job in Kansas, it is revealed that you have a limiting belief that caps how much income you can make without causing a major disruption in your life. You recognize the circumstances, situations, and choices you've made that brought you to this point. Once you feel comfortable with the amount of information you obtain (you've reached awareness) you say, "I cancel this *(insert what you would like to cancel)* across all dimensions of space and time. I place this into my Akashic Records, and I Intend for it to be carried out and executed now."

If you would like, add the progression method where you see yourself building your capacity for a higher salary. Visualize this money coming in with ease through increased opportunities and with joy. You may envision yourself going to pick up your check with an additional $10,000 for the month and watch yourself utilize this money in ways that bring joy.

In essence, clearing and resetting in the Akashic Records isn't about instant fixes. It's a deliberate process, intertwining awareness, intention, and progressive action to foster genuine transformation and pave the way for new, empowering choices.

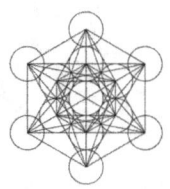

Chapter Notes

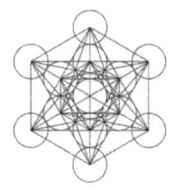

CHAPTER 10

Weaving the Threads of Wisdom: Integrating the Akashic Records into Your Spiritual Journey

"I never want you to do something for me. I want you to do it for yourself—to honor the version of you that desires what is best for you. Remember, knowledge without application is useless. How will you apply what you have learned to enhance the quality of your own life?" - Dr. La Toya Davis

Bringing it All Together

The concept of the Akashic Records has woven itself into the spiritual fabric of humanity throughout history. From ancient civilizations to modern spiritual movements, the idea of a cosmic repository of knowledge and experiences has been embraced across diverse cultures.

Whether through meditation, trance states, or intuitive insights, seekers have attempted to access this infinite reservoir of wisdom to gain deeper understanding and guidance in their spiritual journey. The Records offer a profound opportunity to understand your soul-self, your interconnectedness, and your place within the grand tapestry of existence. On your journey, remember to continue embracing self-healing, growth, and empowerment while respecting the sanctity of the Records and the profound insights they offer.

As you continue to build your relationship with the Records, keep in mind that you are exploring a soul-level perspective. The information you receive is infused with love and devoid of judgment. As individuated pieces of Source, you do not make mistakes, only choices. Therefore, no judgment clouds your path; instead, love guides you.

The choices you make serve as opportunities for growth, learning, and understanding. The Akashic Records can help you comprehend the reasons behind your choices, assess their impact, and inspire any necessary shifts or changes. The Records are a tool for understanding, healing, and elevating yourself, not a place to intrude into someone else's privacy or to cause harm.

Despite the vastness of the Akashic Records, they do not serve as a crystal ball for predicting the future. The future is an amalgamation of countless possibilities, making it challenging to pinpoint a single outcome. Instead, the Records offer insights into the potentials that exist at any given moment.

Using the Akashic Records, you can seek guidance for any aspect of your life. It is an ever-present realm of light and wisdom, accessible day or night. Whether navigating challenging experiences, considering career choices, or seeking alignment with personal goals, the Records hold infinite possibilities.

Three key concepts guide you toward a successful experience: trust the process, resist doubt, and embrace the judgment-free nature of the guidance received. The realm of the Akashic Records is devoid of negativity or harmful entities seeking to deceive or mislead.

No Room for Fear

In the Akashic Records, there is no room for fear or self-criticism. Unlike the critical inner voice you may experience in your daily life, the Records greet you with unconditional love and non-judgmental wisdom. Even if you enter the Records with certain choices or experiences you may not be proud of, you need not worry about judgment or criticism. The Records will provide guidance and insights without condemnation, allowing you to move forward on your journey.

Guidance, Not Control

Within the Akashic Records, you do not receive outright directives or commands. Do not seek answers to should-I-do questions. Instead, the Records provide guidance that can support you in making our choices with clarity and wisdom. You will always retain your free will and ability to choose, with the Records respecting and supporting your decisions.

A Developing Relationship

Your interaction with the Records is like building a relationship. It is a process that grows and deepens over time, much like a muscle strengthened through regular exercise. As you engage with the Records more frequently, you become more adept at interpreting and understanding the guidance you receive.

Fixed and Evolving Aspects

When seeking information in the Akashic Records, you encounter two types: fixed and evolving aspects. Fixed aspects represent your blueprint, the unchanging vibrational aspects of yourself. On the other hand, evolving aspects reflect choices you make throughout your lifetimes, including decisions on careers, relationships, and life experiences.

Accessible to All

Contrary to misconceptions, accessing the Akashic Records does not require psychic abilities or out-of-body experiences. It is a process open to everyone willing to learn and invest effort in their spiritual journey. Each one of us possesses various forms of spiritual senses, or Claires, which can be developed and honed to connect with spiritual information beyond our physical perception.

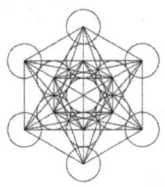

Chapter Notes

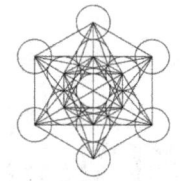

Additional Notes

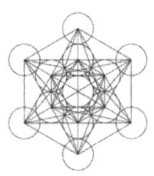

Final Thoughts

Thanks for embarking on this transformative journey through the realms of the Akashic Records with me. Now that you've reached the end of the book, take a moment to acknowledge the courage and commitment it took to explore the depths of your soul and the mysteries of the universe. You have shown resilience, curiosity, and a willingness to expand your consciousness beyond the confines of the known.

In your quest to uncover the wisdom held within the Akashic Records, you tapped into a wellspring of knowledge that transcends time and space. Through the guidance of the Masters, Teachers, and Loved Ones, you gained insights into your past, clarity for your present, and vision for your future. You discovered that you are the architect of your destiny, and the Akashic Records are the blueprint from which you can create a life of purpose, meaning, and fulfillment.

As you continue on your journey, remember that the path to self-discovery is not always linear or easy. There may be challenges, doubts, and moments of uncertainty along the way. But know that you are never alone. The wisdom of the Akashic Records is always available to guide you, support you, and remind you of your inherent worth and potential.

Embrace each experience as an opportunity for growth and expansion. Trust in the unfolding of your journey, knowing that every twist and turn has a purpose and a lesson to teach. Cultivate gratitude for the blessings that surround you and for the miracles that manifest in your life.

Above all, remember that you are a divine being, capable of infinite love, wisdom, and compassion. You are here to shine your light brightly and to contribute your unique gifts to the world. The Akashic Records are a sacred tool to help you remember your true essence and to live in alignment with your soul's highest purpose.

So, as you close this book and step forward into the next chapter of your journey, do so with confidence, grace, and a sense of wonder. May you continue to explore the depths of your soul, follow the guidance of your heart, and embody the limitless potential that resides within you.

Thank you for joining me on this journey. May the wisdom of the Akashic Records continue to illuminate your path and inspire you to live your most extraordinary life.

Appendix A

OPENING FOR SELF:

I give thanks to the Masters, Teachers, Loved Ones, and Keepers of the Akashic Record for preserving the sanctity of the Akashic field. At this time, I intend to enter into my Akashic Records. With a clear mind and a pure heart, I come to receive information in alignment with achieving my highest good on this plane and my Soul's journey. *Remove from me any self-centeredness or remnants of ego that would cause conflict with receiving information in the light of love from which it flows.* Attune me instantly to the highest vibration for clarity, love, light, and elevation.

Thank you. Thank you. Thank you.

The Records are Now Open.

CLOSING FOR SELF:

Thank you to the Masters, Teachers, Loved Ones, and Keepers of the Akashic Record for sharing wisdom and energy with me today. As I close my records, may the energetic exchange of healing and guidance continue to resonate. Thank you, Thank you, Thank you.

The Records are Now Closed.

To download your copy of the Akashic Key Process, visit www.learnakashic. com/book.

Appendix B

EXAMPLE QUESTIONS

Here are a few questions to help you navigate and understand the ways that your soul is most in alignment with the ways it chose to live this lifetime.

1. How did I choose to experience life in this incarnation?
2. What is a soul-level trait that I have?
3. What are my inherent divine gifts and talents?
4. How can I best share my divine gifts and talents with others?
5. What is the main life lesson for me in this lifetime?
6. What area of my life can I pay more attention to that will bring me greater (peace, happiness, abundance, ease, fulfillment, joy)?
7. What past life experiences are repeating themselves at this moment?
8. What mental blocks are preventing me from walking more confidently in my purpose?
9. What is one thing I can do to lead a soul-led life?
10. What does my day look/feel like when I am in alignment with my path?

Appendix C

Blockage Resolution Protocol

Before going into the Akashic Records, ask yourself these questions:

    1). What is my current situation?

    2). What is the ideal successful resolution of this situation?

    3). Why would this new outcome be better?

While in your Records, you work to identify information in these areas:

    1). What is the root cause of the situation/challenge?

    2). What do I need to let go/release/stop doing as it relates to this situation?

    3). What qualities/characteristics do I need to bring into my life to bring about the successful resolution?

    4). What new actions/behaviors/habits/systems do I need to put in place or take to move me into alignment with my desires?

The following are example questions appropriate for each step while in your Records. Remember, these are only examples, and you can adjust the questions to fit your particular circumstance.

Step 1 – Example Root Cause Questions:

What do I need to understand about my relationship with my coworkers?

What exactly don't I like about my job?

Why is my business losing money?

What am I ignoring in relation to my work/business/relationship that would be helpful to acknowledge?

What is stopping me from pursuing my dreams?

Where am I stuck in my relationship with_____?

What is my current relationship with_____teaching me?

What do I offer and receive in my relationship with_____?

What is the dynamic of my relationship with_____?

How do _____and I support each other in growth both in the relationship and individually?

Step 2 – Example Let Go/Release Questions:

What patterns or behaviors am I engaged in that are blocking my gifts?

What can I shift or release to get my work/business/relationship moving?

What do I need to let go of to improve my relationship with_____?

What connections are there between this and any past life experiences?

What are some limiting beliefs and ideas I inherited from my family that are keeping me_____?

What beliefs and ideas have I internalized from my culture that are hindering me from_____?

Step 3 – Example Becoming Questions:

What does my day look like when I am in alignment with my soul purpose?

What qualities do I need to work on in order to increase my ability to earn and maintain money?

What habits should I include in order to become in alignment with the frequency of love?

What qualities do I need to embody to be more effective as a father/mother/husband/wife/etc?

What can I understand, release or shift to find deeper understanding about _____?

Step 4 – Example Action/Implementation Questions:

What can I do to create a life of fulfillment?

What actions can I take to align with my soul purpose?

What skills or talents are in highest alignment for me to focus on developing to help me achieve my life's purpose?

What can I do to create a life of fulfillment?

How can I use my talents to serve others?

What can I do to create more joy and fulfillment in my work?

How can I better service my clients/customers?

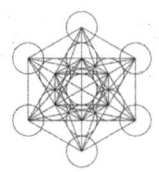

References

Blavatsky, H. P. (1888). *The secret doctrine: The synthesis of science, religion, and philosophy* (Vols. 1-2). Theosophical Publishing Company.

Pagels, E. (1979). *The Gnostic gospels*. Random House.

Steiner, R. (1959). *Cosmic memory: Prehistory of earth and man.* Rudolf Steiner Publications.

Stinnett, A. P. (1883). *Esoteric Buddhism*. Trübner & Co.

Sugrue, T. (1945). There is a river: The story of Edgar Cayce. A.S. Barnes and Company.